The Fourteen Holy Helpers

Publisher's note

Although the term "Holy Helpers" refers to the Christian saints, the tradition of invocation is much older. As Christianity spread, it adopted and renamed all kinds of ancient lore and their associated powers, in much the same way as churches were generally built on pre-Christian religious sites. We can therefore assume that the powers we call upon have little to do with these particular historical figures but instead correspond to primordial energies that reside within humans and the Earth. It is perfectly acceptable to address them by their commonly known Christian names and indeed learn more about their character from the legends of the saints, but people who are in no way aligned with Christianity can just as successfully practice invocation.

the Fourteen Holy Helpers

Invocations for Healing and Protection

Christiane Stamm

EARTHDANCER

AN INNER TRADITIONS IMPRINT

Disclaimer
The author and publishers accept no liability for the practices described in this book. Neither the author nor the publishers shall be liable for any damages that may arise from using the methods and advice set out in the book. Consult your doctor or alternative practitioner in the event of any health concerns. The practice of using invocation can never replace visiting a physician. The prayers of healing cannot be used as an exclusive treatment method. Use invocation only as a complementary method for additional healing.

First edition 2022
The Fourteen Holy Helpers
Invocations for Healing and Protection
Christiane Stamm

This English edition © 2022 Earthdancer GmbH
English translation © 2022 JMS books LLP
Editing by JMS books LLP (www.jmseditorial.com)

Originally published in German as: *Besprechen mit den 14 Nothelfern*
World © 2019, Neue Erde GmbH, Saarbruecken, Germany

Cover design: Aaron Davis; DesignIsIdentity.com
Cover images: 123RF.com
Typesetting and layout: Chris Bell
Typeset in Palatino LT
Crystal drawings throughout: shutterstock.com © masmas
Printed and bound in the United States by Versa Press, Inc.

MIX
Paper from
responsible sources
FSC
www.fsc.org
FSC® C005010

ISBN 978-1-64411-469-8 (print)
ISBN 978-1-64411-470-4 (ebook)

Published by Earthdancer, an imprint of Inner Traditions
www.earthdancerbooks.com, www.innertraditions.com

Contents

Using the Prayers of Healing

My mission

MANY YEARS AGO, I received an instruction from the spirit world to revise the ancient prayers connected to the Fourteen Holy Helpers and to offer them to humanity through initiation.

It was not an easy task, as I was only familiar with the old, rather garbled texts that were almost impossible to recite. It was impressed upon me in no uncertain terms that I should never use any negative words or phrases when formulating the texts and I began my efforts to revise them. After many failed attempts, the spirit world came to my aid and passed on to me the exact prayers. Once healing crystals to accompany the prayers had also been recommended, the invocations finally became effective and it was possible to help people with them.

When I asked why it should be now, at this precise moment, that I had received the instruction to revise these ancient prayers, the answer came that it was now time to make invocation accessible to everyone, since all human and spiritual beings draw their energy from one and the same Source.

Invocation can be passed on to another person on any *day of a full moon*.

Do you want to be healthy?

WHEN ASKED, people will naturally reply that of course they would like to be blessed with perfect health and well-being, but how often during a conversation does talk turn instead to disease, to the things that people don't want? If a sick person wishes to be healed, they must direct their focus, their entire energy, toward good health. The same principle applies in all areas of life.

- If you concentrate on something unpleasant, bad things will happen.

- If you focus your attention on beauty, health, and well-being, most of these good things will come to pass.

- If you would like to be healthy, make a determined and final decision to be healthy and keep to it.

- Consciously forego any potential advantages of sickness and be resolute in this respect.

- Never underestimate the power of the spoken word, since your soul will respond to it.

- You would like to have good health, so resolve never to use the word "sickness" again.

The Fourteen Holy Helpers

THE FOURTEEN HOLY HELPERS were being invoked and worshiped as early as the 9th century, but they have increasingly fallen into obscurity in contemporary times. Their help was particularly vital in the 13th and 14th centuries, when plague reigned supreme throughout the world. It was during this period that the Holy Helpers were especially important.

Each of the Fourteen Holy Helpers was also assigned additional areas of responsibility, and people would call upon a specific saint for help in times of crisis. In so doing the Holy Helpers would address the temporal and spiritual problems of the age.

As a result of globalization and the breakneck pace of technological and scientific advances, especially in medicine, we have gradually become less familiar with the saints in our everyday lives. In reality, little has changed over the centuries, although the precise issues that people are concerned about may now be different—instead of plague, there is cancer or AIDS, and of course COVID-19. Instead of famine, there are job losses and unemployment, so the need right now for angels, saints, and the Fourteen Holy Helpers is as great as ever.

Although over many long centuries people would invoke the Holy Helpers to assist them with their troubles and concerns, the cult surrounding them only garnered recognition thanks to an apparition. Legend has it that the "Fourteen" appeared to a local man, Hermann Leicht, in what is now Klosterlangheim in Upper Franconia, Germany, identifying themselves as the Fourteen Holy Helpers. Hermann Leicht was a shepherd in the town of Langheim when this took place in 1445 and 1446. A chapel was initially built on the site of the visitation, and in 1774 German architect Balthasar Neumann built the Basilica of the Fourteen Holy Helpers, which went on to become a popular pilgrimage site.

The Fourteen Holy Helpers are generally said to comprise:

Saint Agathius (Acacius of Byzantium)

Saint Barbara

Saint Blaise (Blase)

Saint Catherine of Alexandria

Saint Christopher

Saint Cyriacus

Saint Denis (Dionysius)

Saint Erasmus (Elmo)

Saint Eustace (Placidus)

Saint George

Saint Giles (Gilles)

Saint Margaret of Antioch (Marina the Great Martyr)

Saint Pantaleon (Panteleimon)

Saint Vitus (Guy)

In many chronicles, the Four Holy Marshals are also included:

Saint Anthony the Great

Saint Hubert, bishop of Liège

Pope Cornelius

Quirinus of Neuss

The first documented mention of the Four Marshals, also known as the Holy Marshals, was in 1478. However, by the end of the 17th century, depictions of the marshals were becoming less common and veneration of them eventually died away.

An invocation may be addressed to one of the Fourteen Holy Helpers for a number of reasons, while prayers of healing are generally recited to restore health.

The subject of an invocation may also be a physical object such as an amulet, a house or apartment, or indeed a crystal to be carried as a good luck charm and symbol of support. Alternatively, an idea or concept, or a relationship such as a partnership could also be the subject of an invocation. For more details, see the *Using the Prayers of Healing* chapter, on page 47.

Initiation

IN PRINCIPLE, anyone can learn invocation, since we are all part of the same energy. Therefore, everyone can bring help and healing through invocation. In its perfected form, it is natural magic, which is why it has been interpreted as magical and considered mystical since the earliest times. According to ancient tradition, spiritual knowledge and its attendant rituals must be passed on from one person to another. This used to be carried out by word of mouth, from master to pupil, but in this day and age we also make use of the medium of the written word.

This process of handing on knowledge (initiation) and the passages in this book will connect you with the energy of secret knowledge; its power will live within you. After following the instructions, you will be initiated exactly as if you had received this knowledge from your ancestors.

You now have some work to do—there is no such thing as something for nothing! You will need a pad of blank paper to use as a personal journal, or you might like to choose a nice notebook, but wait for the next full moon before beginning to copy out your prayers of healing. It is only in the act of copying out the prayers that the magic of invocation will pass to you. Discover more in the *Using the Prayers of Healing* chapter, page 47.

The Prayers of Invocation and Healing

The Fourteen Holy Helpers

O, Fourteen Holy Helpers
banish wounds and hurt.
May evil be banished
and love enter the heart.

O, Fourteen Holy Helpers
banish wounds and hurt.
May evil be banished
and love enter the heart.

O, Fourteen Holy Helpers
banish wounds and hurt.
May evil be banished
and love enter the heart.
So shall it be!
In the name of the Father, and of the Son,
and of the Holy Spirit.
Amen.

Evil is banished and good summoned with this cleansing prayer.

Joy in life shall be yours.

All Fourteen Holy Helpers are entreated to program your body for good health.

Recite this prayer of healing at the beginning of every invocation.

Helps with:

- finding joy in life again
- depression
- anxiety
- protection
- sorrow
- psychosis
- nightmares

Healing crystal
Clear quartz (clarity)

Wearing or being close to clear quartz brings clarity and the insight to see yourself more clearly, recognizing what is real and true. At the same time, it awakens primordial instincts, preparing you to find the way to inner truth. It helps to remove blockages that cause many diseases.

Saint Christopher

You, Saint Christopher,
and all the Holy Helpers above,
touch the wound with love;
with my hand remove the pain,
and bring goodness to my heart again.

You, Saint Christopher,
and all the Holy Helpers above,
touch the wound with love;
with my hand remove the pain,
and bring goodness to my heart again.

You, Saint Christopher,
and all the Holy Helpers above,
touch the wound with love;
with my hand remove the pain,
and bring goodness to my heart again.
So shall it be!
In the name of the Father, and of the Son,
and of the Holy Spirit.
Amen.

Helps with:

- wounds
- migraines
- acute and chronic pain
- toothache
- palpitations, heart failure, angina
- neuralgia
- eye conditions

Healing crystal
Obsidian (snowflake obsidian)

Obsidian helps to interrupt and disrupt old, entrenched attitudes and thought patterns. Painful memories will dissolve and disappear, and positive thinking will be stimulated within the subconscious once more. You will be more immediately aware of your talents and abilities, and will be able to develop these freely once more. Obsidian is also known as the first-aid crystal.

Saint Blaise

Torment, inflammation, anguish,
heal,
leave the body.
Allow goodness to enter,
and may strong health we feel.

Torment, inflammation, anguish,
heal,
leave the body.
Allow goodness to enter,
and may strong health we feel.

Torment, inflammation, anguish,
heal,
leave the body.
Allow goodness to enter,
and may strong health we feel.
So shall it be!
In the name of the Father, and of the Son,
and of the Holy Spirit.
Amen.

Helps with:

- pain
- inflammation (skin and joints)
- coughs, bronchitis, asthma, sore throat, earache
- itching
- neurodermatitis
- nervous disorders
- convulsions
- allergies

Healing crystal
Chalcedony

Chalcedony is known as the stone of orators and encourages openness. It supports self-expression and communication, bringing a certain sense of ease to life for the wearer. It helps to disrupt old patterns of behavior and attitudes and dissolve blockages.

Saint Margaret of Antioch

Saint Margaret, heal the wound
unbound.
May blood be still,
swelling subside again,
And begone, all pain.

St Margaret, heal the wound
unbound.
May blood be still,
swelling subside again,
And begone, all pain.

St Margaret, heal the wound
unbound.
May blood be still,
swelling subside again,
And begone, all pain.
So shall it be!
In the name of the Father, and of the Son,
and of the Holy Spirit.
Amen.

Helps with:

- accelerated healing of broken bones
- wound healing
- acne, boils
- menstrual complaints
- infertility
- menopause
- controlling bleeding

Healing crystal
Rose quartz

Rose quartz brings trust and love of one's neighbor. It promotes a sense of peace in the soul. The inner self, often a heart that has grown hard, will relent and soften, allowing harmony to prevail once more.

Saint Catherine of Alexandria

Saint Catherine fights death,
three roses in her hand:
the first is white,
the second red,
the third brings harmony in its stead.

Saint Catherine fights death,
three roses in her hand:
the first is white,
the second red,
the third brings harmony in its stead.

Saint Catherine fights death,
three roses in her hand:
the first is white,
the second red,
the third brings harmony in its stead.
So shall it be!
In the name of the Father, and of the Son,
and of the Holy Spirit.
Amen.

Helps with:

- herpes-related conditions
- shingles
- chicken pox
- breast cancer
- cysts
- speech impediments (stuttering, for example)

Healing crystal
Lapis lazuli

Lapis lazuli helps those who wear it to express unspoken and long-repressed issues. Wear it for a lengthy period and you will be able to give voice to any issues that have been troubling you clearly and rationally, without excessive emotion. The stone of truth, it also restores strength of faith and delivers inspiration, wisdom, and intuition.

Saint Barbara

Saint Barbara, cleanse the blood,
restore its balance,
make all well and good.
So may it be.

Saint Barbara, cleanse the blood,
restore its balance,
make all well and good.
So may it be.

Saint Barbara, cleanse the blood,
restore its balance,
make all well and good.
So may it be.
So shall it be!
In the name of the Father, and of the Son,
and of the Holy Spirit.
Amen.

This prayer is used in all invocations.

Helps with:

- acidosis (hyperacidity) of the blood
- detoxification of the body
- boosting the immune system
- AIDS, cancer, rheumatism, diabetes

The sixth prayer is the optimum prayer for any form of healing.

It has a positive effect on the pH value of the blood and stimulates the detoxification process.

Healing crystal
Heliotrope (bloodstone)

Heliotrope is one of the so-called "healing stones" of Saint Hildegard of Bingen. It helps the wearer to maintain their composure no matter what happens in life. It alleviates irritability and deflects negative energies. It fortifies the immune system and is described as the echinacea (or cure-all) of healing crystals as a result.

Saint George

Saint George, strengthen the body.
May heat and fire be banned,
removed by your holy hand.

Saint George, strengthen the body
May heat and fire be banned,
removed by your holy hand.

Saint George, strengthen the body.
May heat and fire be banned,
removed by your holy hand.
So shall it be!
In the name of the Father, and of the Son,
and of the Holy Spirit.
Amen.

Helps with:

- high fever
- frostbite
- burns

Healing crystal
Prase

Prase helps to calm tension and reduce aggression. It encourages the wearer to lead a self-determined life and helps them to keep a cool head in situations of conflict. One of the crystals used as a healing stone by Saint Hildegard of Bingen, it also helps those who have quarreled to reconcile.

Saint Pantaleon

Wart that I touch, disappear.
Wart that I see, begone from here.
Heal for all eternity.
Strengthen the body.

Wart that I touch, disappear.
Wart that I see, begone from here.
Heal for all eternity.
Strengthen the body.

Wart that I touch, disappear.
Wart that I see, begone from here.
Heal for all eternity.
Strengthen the body.
So shall it be!
In the name of the Father, and of the Son,
and of the Holy Spirit.
Amen.

Helps with:

- plantar warts
- genital warts
- hand warts
- myomas (uterine fibroids)
- cysts

Healing crystal
Amethyst

Amethyst boosts concentration and promotes clarity and wisdom, bringing greater vigor and vitality. Placing an amethyst under your pillow at night will help you to enjoy a more relaxed and refreshing sleep. This crystal is considered a protective "radiation stone" that may counter the effects of electrosmog.

Saint Denis

Eczema, sorrows of the soul,
all inner turmoil, heal.
Itching, for ever begone.
Body be strengthened again.

Eczema, sorrows of the soul,
all inner turmoil, heal.
Itching, for ever begone.
Body be strengthened again.

Eczema, sorrows of the soul,
all inner turmoil, heal.
Itching, for ever begone.
Body be strengthened again.
So shall it be!
In the name of the Father, and of the Son,
and of the Holy Spirit.
Amen.

Helps with:

- mental suffering
- inner turmoil
- neurodermatitis
- psoriasis
- all eczema conditions

Healing crystal
Jade

Jade boosts physical performance and creates the balance that we need in life. It enhances reactions, especially in those involved in dangerous professions. Jade also brings cheerfulness and exerts a calming influence.

Saint Cyriacus

Inflammation and rash;
drive all things out.
I implore you:
leave the place you find yourself now.

Inflammation and rash,
drive all things out.
I implore you:
leave the place you find yourself now.

Inflammation and rash,
drive all things out.
I implore you:
leave the place you find yourself now.
So shall it be!
In the name of the Father, and of the Son,
and of the Holy Spirit.
Amen.

Helps with:

- animal diseases

- erysipelas (skin infection)

- allergic skin reactions

- phlebitis (vein inflammation)

Healing crystal
Agate

Agate supports concentration and exerts a harmonizing influence. It also has a protective effect, as it stimulates memory and promotes peace to heal "old" mental wounds. Agate brings renewed courage.

Saint Eustace

Bites, stings, burns,
And nettle rash, leave without trace.
Away, take flight from this place.

Bites, stings, burns,
And nettle rash, leave without trace.
Away, take flight from this place.

Bites, stings, burns,
And nettle rash, leave without trace.
Away, take flight from this place.
So shall it be!
In the name of the Father, and of the Son,
and of the Holy Spirit.
Amen.

Helps with:

- burns
- nettle rash
- drug intolerance
- sunburn
- wasp and bee stings
- all allergies

Healing crystal
Rhodonite

Rhodonite helps you to reach a point at which you can accept and tolerate change (such as a new job or moving house) more easily. It promotes self-actualization and encourages you to allow more joy and confidence into your life. The so-called "examination crystal," rhodonite is very useful for children and young people taking exams, when it can help to ease any associated anxiety.

Saint Agathius

Painful joints,
inflammation of the bone,
be soothed, heal soon.
And may this suffering never return.

Painful joints,
inflammation of the bone,
be soothed, heal soon.
And may this suffering never return.

Painful joints
inflammation of the bone,
be soothed, heal soon.
And may this suffering never return.
So shall it be!
In the name of the Father, and of the Son,
and of the Holy Spirit.
Amen.

Helps with:

- back pain
- lumbago
- vertebral conditions
- all complaints affecting the spinal column
- Scheuermann's disease (curve of upper back)
- pectus excavatum (funnel chest)
- ankylosing spondylitis (chronic arthritis in the spine)

Healing crystal
Smoky quartz

Smoky quartz is suitable for those who work hard and helps to release tension. It also helps the wearer to be less resistant to things. It is perfect for meditation and for staying well-grounded in Mother Earth. Smoky quartz is seen as an anti-stress crystal.

Saint Giles

Waxing moon,
drives the water hence
from every channel
all at once.

Waxing moon
drives the water hence
from every channel
all at once.

Waxing moon
drives the water hence
from every channel
all at once.
So shall it be!
In the name of the Father, and of the Son,
and of the Holy Spirit.
Amen.

Helps with:

- epilepsy
- edemas (water retention)
- lymphostasis (disruption in lymphatic circulation)
- dropsy

Healing crystal
Howlite

Howlite helps you to make and carry out plans. It challenges you to take better control of your life, especially if you have a tendency to lose sight of your projects and goals. It redresses balance.

Saint Erasmus

Erasmus, bring with you the sun.
Illness, shrivel and dry out; healing and love come.
May sunshine return
to a happy home (the body).

Erasmus, bring with you the sun.
Illness, shrivel and dry out; healing and love come.
May sunshine return
to a happy home (the body).

Erasmus, bring with you the sun.
Illness, shrivel and dry out; healing and love come.
May sunshine return
to a happy home (the body).
So shall it be!
In the name of the Father, and of the Son,
and of the Holy Spirit.
Amen.

Helps with:

- spreading growths of all kinds
- tumors
- myomas (fibroids)
- cysts
- ulcers
- cramps
- colic
- stomach complaints
- addictions

Healing crystals
Azurite-malachite

Azurite-malachite protects the wearer from mental instability, which can often be a root cause of serious illness. It helps to resolve inner conflicts in good time, opening people up to the world and those around them. Azurite-malachite creates a radiant aura and provides the strength to overcome suffering and pain more easily.

Tiger iron or tiger's eye

Tiger iron works quickly to combat tiredness and exhaustion. It is seen as an energy crystal and provides strength and vitality, delivering stamina and allowing the wearer to act speedily when necessary. It resolves a variety of blockages and restores mental balance. Tiger's eye can also be used as an alternative, although its iron content is lower.

Saint Vitus

Limbs trembling,
daily, life in agony.
May peace succeed and suffering recede.
Light and love for eternity.

Limbs trembling,
daily, life in agony.
May peace succeed and suffering recede.
Light and love for eternity.

Limbs trembling,
daily, life in agony.
May peace succeed and suffering recede.
Light and love for eternity.
So shall it be!
In the name of the Father, and of the Son,
and of the Holy Spirit.
Amen.

Helps with:

- cramps
- Parkinson's disease
- epilepsy

Healing crystal
Rutilated quartz

Rutilated quartz works like an antidepressant. It fosters and supports new hopes and ideas, making worries and cares less burdensome. It brings people new confidence and flashes of inspiration, which can manifest as visions of future life. It lifts the mood and resolves all forms of blockages. Energy is able to flow freely once more and the body becomes more active.

Using the Prayers of Healing

IN ORDER FOR INITIATION to be successful, it is essential to copy out the prayers you require in your own hand and in your own notebook or journal, exactly in accordance with the prescribed ritual. Once everything has been carried out as specified, you will be initiated, and all the power and energy of the prayers will be available to you.

When writing out the prayers during the initiation process, some people report experiencing a sensation of warmth or a tingling throughout their whole body, along with feelings of love for others as well as for themselves. However, this may not necessarily be the case for you, since reactions differ from person to person.

Please remember the following:

- During an invocation, the most important requirement is to be calm and focused.

- Never carry out invocation when you are under time pressure or feeling stressed.

- Take your time and wait until you feel completely relaxed and entirely at ease, safe, and secure.

- Now, allow yourself to be guided step-by-step and you will learn how to use healing prayers correctly.

Read through each prayer in your head several times, repeating each time:

In the name of the Father, and of the Son,
and of the Holy Spirit.
Amen.

This sentence can also be adapted and the prayer said in the name of Allah, or of the Universe, or in the name of Light or of Love—do what feels right for you. However, do not alter the phrase "**so shall it be**" under any circumstances. If you were to do so, you would sacrifice the power of the energetic flow, since this is an ancient phrase with great inherent power and energy. Recite it slowly and with all your heart in order to allow it to develop its full strength and power.

At this point, I recommend that you learn the first prayer of the Fourteen Holy Helpers and the sixth prayer to Saint Barbara by heart, since you will need these prayers for every invocation.

Invocation procedure
for personal use

Make yourself comfortable, either lying on a bed or seated in an armchair.

Relax and adjust your position until you feel at ease.

Place both hands on your solar plexus (level with your stomach); put your left hand in position first, and then place your right hand over your left.

Make sure your hands are about a hand's width above your navel, or place your hands directly on the area you wish to treat.

Your eyes may be open or closed.

Now focus all your attention on the first prayer and recite it:

O, Fourteen Holy Helpers.

You will soon feel the power and energy released by this prayer of healing flowing through your hands. The feeling will last for several minutes and your whole body will be flooded with energy. When you sense that it is beginning to subside, this is an indication that the body has "refueled" and absorbed sufficient energy for the time being.

CHECKING THE RESULTS

Hold your hands around 4 inches (10 cm) above your solar plexus or the area of the body to be treated. Repeat the first prayer (O, Fourteen Holy Helpers). You should now feel a pleasant, warm energy and an invigorating power.

DEALING WITH UNSATISFACTORY RESULTS

Should you fail to experience warmth and good feelings, it could be the result of a number of factors:

- Were you interrupted by something: the telephone, doorbell, children…?
- Did you have difficulty concentrating?
- Did you find it hard to relax?
- Did you encounter any difficulties with the text when reciting the prayer, perhaps stumbling over or mixing up sentences?
- Did you suddenly find yourself worrying about something?

If you are still unsuccessful after several attempts, try starting again from the very beginning.

If you still do not succeed, try allowing someone else to carry out an initiation. However, if there is no possibility of carrying out an initiation with the help of a third party, do get in touch with me. My contact details are in the appendix.

Do not forget that we all share the same energy source on this Earth. Proceed in faith. You **can** learn how to perform an invocation. That is precisely the purpose of this book.

Once you have completed a successful dress rehearsal or trial, you can start to work with other people. However, before using your skills to help others, it is recommended that you find a number of people who are prepared to be test subjects. Of course, both you and the person being treated in this capacity will experience the flow of power and energy.

After around ten to fifteen sessions, you will find that your sensitivity and empathy have developed, and your faith and confidence will have grown as the power of invocation flows through your hands and the energy of the prayers of healing takes effect.

- If you are laying on hands for yourself, you will feel tingling or warmth. If you are treating others, the energy will be noticeably stronger.

- When performing an invocation, you can either lay your hands directly on the body or hold them around 4 inches (10 cm) above it. This does not affect the power and energy of the prayers of healing.

- If laying on hands for someone who is ill or is suffering, the energy will flow first through you and then through their body to resolve their health issues.

- If treating yourself, you will experience a tingling or slight warmth.

- If treating someone else, you may be surprised to notice how much stronger the flow of energy is.

Therapy with the prayers of healing

THE FIRST PRAYER of healing (O, Fourteen Holy Helpers) is used in every invocation, as the energy of this prayer opens up mind, body, and soul for healing. You will experience feelings of cheerfulness, lightness, and happiness, which is necessary for all healing.

Work according to your feelings or the given situation. It is important that both you and the person you are working with feel at ease; the position that they adopt for the treatment is less crucial—for example, they may be seated. Now lay your hands on the patient's instep (the upper part of the foot, reaching down to the base of the toes).

Always bear one thing in mind, however—the person being treated should remain quite still and must not move around or fidget in any way. Explain clearly to them that you are not using any sleight of hand and that no "hocus-pocus" or magic tricks for the purposes of entertainment are involved. If you feel they do not have the right attitude, do not carry on with the procedure.

Now, in your mind, recite three times **the three verses of the prayer of healing (O, Fourteen Holy Helpers)** as it is written out in your journal. Keep your hands on the person's feet for around five minutes.

This prayer of healing is recited for every invocation (treatment).

Once the five minutes have ended, remove your hands from their feet. Place one hand (left or right) on their solar plexus (a hand's width above the navel), then place the other on their lower back.

Leave your hands in position as you recite the sixth prayer of healing (Saint Barbara). It is important for the healing process, since it detoxifies and deacidifies the body. After reciting the prayer, leave your hands in position for several more minutes. Recite the Saint Barbara prayer just as you did the first prayer: **three verses, three times**.

This prayer of healing is recited for every invocation (procedure).

After reciting the prayer, leave your hands in position on the solar plexus and lower back for several minutes and feel the healing energy of the prayer.

Leave your hands in position on the body or move them to the part of the body to be treated.

Now recite the prayer of healing that relates to the issue you wish to address. Recite the three verses just once.

Please do not be concerned that you might make an error when carrying out an invocation. The people you are working with (and you, yourself) will absorb only the energy of the prayers of healing.

Once the treatment has been completed, leave your hands in position for several minutes.

If you have been treating yourself, once you have finished, remove your hands but do not stand up yet. Remain in your relaxed position for several more minutes before standing up again. It can take up to ten minutes before you feel your normal energy levels returning.

To help the invocation to run smoothly, I recommend that you learn the opening prayer (O, Fourteen Holy Helpers) and the sixth prayer (Saint Barbara) by heart, until you are able to recite them perfectly and with warmth and sincerity.

Sequence of prayers
of healing

THE FIRST PRAYER of healing (O, Fourteen Holy Helpers) is always recited at the beginning of a session. It will prepare your body and your energy for healing and awaken your vitality.

Similarly, the sixth prayer (Saint Barbara) is also always recited. It is essential for balancing out the acid levels in the blood. It also helps to detoxify the body and plays a crucial preliminary role in a positive healing process.

Now recite the prayer that is appropriate to the issue that you wish to address.

Sequence of prayers:

First prayer: O, Fourteen Holy Helpers
(recite the three verses, three times);

Second prayer: Saint Barbara
(recite the three verses, three times);

continue with the third prayer of healing: as appropriate to the issue at hand
(recite the three verses once).

Treatment examples

A KNOWLEDGE **of which prayer of healing to use for which issue is very important.** On the following pages you will find a number of conditions, minor aches and pains that can be treated through invocation. People become ill for a reason, however; always remember that almost every illness has some form of psychological cause. The magic of invocation merely allows you to combat and eliminate symptoms without investigating them or delving into them more deeply. In this respect, the process of invocation does not go far enough and the cause of the illness should also be sought.

Sometimes an honest conversation with the other person is enough to help them to make a decision or change their life in some way, but be careful not act in a patronizing fashion. Everyone has to decide and act for themselves.

Never make your own diagnoses. You must leave that to the physicians. Do not perform an invocation for unexplained, unfocused pain that could be caused by many things. Leave the investigation of such complaints to a doctor. You can always carry out an invocation to complement a medical treatment.

Some people suffer from more than one disease, so it is extremely important for their recovery that you treat each of their complaints with your invocation. But take care. Do not address all their issues at once but instead look at each one separately. This will avoid spreading your energy too thinly and the slow path of convalescence that could result.

WARTS

The eighth prayer (Saint Pantaleon) is used for warts.

Sequence for the invocation:

> Carry out an invocation with the first prayer of healing (O, Fourteen Holy Helpers)
> (recite the three verses, three times);
>
> continue with the sixth prayer of healing (Saint Barbara)
> (recite the three verses, three times);
>
> and finish with the eighth prayer of healing (Saint Pantaleon)
> (recite the three verses once).

Perform this invocation once a week for at least three weeks. It is advisable to repeat an invocation several times in the case of acute complaints.

FEVERISH COLD

Symptoms: pain, fever, inflammation, catarrh, coughs, sniffles.

Sequence for the invocation:

> Carry out an invocation with the first prayer of healing (O, Fourteen Holy Helpers)
> (recite the three verses, three times);
>
> continue with the sixth prayer of healing (Saint Barbara)
> (recite the three verses, three times);
>
> follow with the third prayer of healing (Saint Blaise)
> (recite the three verses once);

then the fourth prayer of healing (Saint Margaret of Antioch) (recite the three verses once);

and finish with the seventh prayer of healing (Saint George) (recite the three verses once).

In the case of acute colds, perform three invocations within three days.

INSECT BITES

As a rule, it is sufficient to perform an invocation with the eleventh prayer (Saint Eustace) only. Recite the three verses just once.

Place the amulet or the appropriate healing crystal (rhodonite) on the bite wound.

A single invocation is often sufficient. The insect bite will stop itching and the inflammation will subside or become almost unnoticeable.

However, for multiple stings, such as from wasps, bees, hornets, or poisonous insects, invocation is no substitute for diagnosis and treatment by a doctor. This is also true in the case of allergies.

BURNS (slight or mild only, with no dirt in the wound)

Perform an invocation at once using the eleventh prayer (Saint Eustace). Recite the three verses just once.

In the case of more severe burns, you must call a doctor.

Invocation is particularly suitable as an aid to recovery from a burn.

Please remember that invocation does not replace visiting a physician.

CUTS TO THE SKIN (minor wounds only)

Bleeding is treated with the fourth prayer (Saint Margaret). This prayer of healing is very effective and can also be used for nosebleeds.

In an emergency, when immediate first aid is required, omit the first and sixth prayer; they can be reinstated in subsequent sessions.

The sequence to be used after an emergency invocation is as follows:

Begin with the first prayer (O, Fourteen Holy Helpers)
(recite the three verses, three times);

then the sixth prayer (Saint Barbara)
(recite the three verses, three times);

finish with the fourth prayer of healing (Saint Margaret of Antioch)
(recite the three verses once).

If the condition is acute/painful, perform an invocation immediately and then every three hours until the pain subsides.

As with burns, only treat slight grazes and shallow cuts that are clean; in all other cases, invocation is intended only as a complementary treatment after seeing a doctor.

Remember that invocation does not replace a consultation with a physician. It is a complementary measure.

Invocations can be performed not just for sickness but also for physical objects or entities such as a house or apartment. They can also be performed for an idea, a partnership or a desire for happiness, as well as for an object to be used for protection (see overleaf).

Performing an invocation for an amulet or crystal as a protective talisman

To perform such an invocation, it is essential to have been initiated (or to have initiated yourself) or you may find that your work, although helpful, is less effective than you might have wished.

Begin by cleansing your chosen crystal or amulet (see page 67). Your crystal or amulet will then be neutral.

Now light a candle and hold the amulet (or crystal) in your left hand (traditionally, the side of your heart).

Close your eyes and take a few moments to find peace and stillness.

Recite the three verses of the first prayer (O, Fourteen Holy Helpers) three times, and visualize being bathed in a shining light until you feel safe, secure, and protected.

Once you have done this, take the crystal or amulet in both hands and blow firmly on it, saying out loud (or in your head) "So shall it be."

You can now go about your normal, everyday life once more, knowing your protective amulet has been programmed and that when you touch it, it will provide help in all kinds of situations.

Performing an invocation
for your home

The threshold of a house or apartment marks the point at which you cross from outside to inside. It should, of course, offer protection against thieves and any uninvited guests or unwelcome callers.

In days gone by there was a more general awareness of the symbolic nature of the threshold than there is today. On January 6, the Feast of Epiphany, in Christian regions and in Roman Catholic areas in particular, the custom was to chalk the initials C+M+B on the lintel or upper part of a door to celebrate the three kings Caspar, Melchior, and Balthasar. This was intended to protect the house and household. The protection would last a year and therefore had to be renewed annually.

An invocation for the house, home, and household operates on the same principle. Nothing lasts for ever—for example, however white and clean something may be, it will become gray over time. You should therefore expect a maximum protection period of one year, after which the protection should be renewed.

Using an invocation for this purpose has the advantage of not being tied to the date of January 6, meaning you can choose on which day the invocation is performed.

Ritual

You will need the following:

- a medium-sized bowl (glass or ceramic)
- approximately 10 to 17 ounces (300 to 500 g) of coarse salt, depending on the size of the house or apartment
- several small bowls (one for each room)

Pour the salt into the bowl and hold it in both hands. Take a few moments to calm your thoughts and ask for peace, joy, protection, and harmony for your home.

Now say the first prayer (O, Fourteen Holy Helpers), reciting all three verses three times, then blow gently over the salt and say with fervor "So shall it be."

If you are carrying out an invocation for a house or apartment, or indeed an object belonging to another person, the first prayer (O, Fourteen Holy Helpers) will generally be sufficient. Recite the three verses just once.

Pour some of the protective salt into each of the small bowls and put one in each room; the bowls look very decorative with candles placed inside them. If you would rather not use a bowl, just sprinkle a few grains of the salt in each room (not forgetting rooms such as an attic or cellar). The remainder can be stored in a screw-top glass container. After a year, however, any remaining salt should be disposed of outdoors.

Repeat the invocation ritual approximately once a year.

Planting lavender outside your front door is also a good way of keeping negative energy at bay, as is placing a green fern behind an entrance to your home. You can perform an invocation for the lavender and fern.

Performing an invocation for your partnership

You will need the following:

- two rose quartz crystals (small enough to fit into one hand)
- a photograph of yourself and your partner together, one in which you are both happy

Cleanse the rose quartz crystals as described on page 67. Hold both crystals in your left hand and take a few moments to find some peace and stillness. Visualize yourself and your partner in love, picturing yourselves embracing or kissing, until you sense an overwhelming feeling of being filled with love.

Now say the first prayer (O, Fourteen Holy Helpers), reciting the three verses just once. You can also invite Saint Cornelius or Saint Valentine to help you create joy and harmony in your partnership. Blow firmly on the crystals and think or say aloud "So shall it be."

Gradually resume your daily routine. Place the crystals in front of the photograph of yourself and your partner, or place them in the bedroom, positioning them in such a way that the crystals are touching, remaining in contact with each other.

The Holy Helpers healing amulet

To make a healing amulet, you will need a very thin cord or thread about 20 inches (50 cm) long and the healing crystals listed below. You will also require around 30 small clear quartz beads and 50 crystal fragments with holes that can be threaded. The crystals should have a diameter of around ¼ to ⅓ inch (between 6 and 8 mm). Finally, you will need a large clear quartz with a diameter of approximately ½ to ⅝ inch (12 to 15 mm) to make the clasp of the amulet.

Healing crystals	Holy Helpers
Clear quartz	Fourteen Holy Helpers
Snowflake obsidian	St. Christopher
Chalcedony	St. Blaise
Rose quartz	St. Margaret of Antioch
Lapis lazuli	St. Catherine of Alexandria
Heliotrope	St. Barbara
Prase quartz	St. George
Amethyst	St. Pantaleon
Jade	St. Denis
Agate	St. Cyriacus
Rhodonite	St. Eustace
Smoky quartz	St. Agathius
Howlite	St. Giles
Azurite-malachite, Tiger iron, Tiger's eye	St. Erasmus
Rutilated quartz	St. Vitus

CLEANSING THE CRYSTALS

Having purchased your crystals, they should be cleansed before use. Hold the crystals under running water for as long as you feel is necessary. Spread a pretty cloth across an empty windowsill and arrange the crystals on top of it in the sun. Daylight will be sufficient to achieve a good result so there is no need to be concerned if the sky is overcast. The healing crystals should be left here undisturbed for 24 hours. It is important that they are charged with both sun and moon energy to fully develop your healing powers.

MAKING A HEALING AMULET

Cut a length of cord and tie a thick knot at one end. Then thread the first healing crystal onto the cord, make a knot after the crystal, then thread on a piece of clear quartz, make another knot, then thread on a crystal, and continue in this way until you have a necklace of the required size. The precise order of the healing crystals is not important—this will be your personalized amulet, but the crystals and quartz should always alternate, separated each time by a knot. It can be worn around your neck or carried with you in a special bag. Perhaps hang it behind your front door or keep it in the car as a protective talisman, depending on the specific purpose of your invocation.

If you wish to discharge or reprogram your healing amulet in the future, perform another cleansing.

Activating the Holy Helpers amulet or individual healing crystals

After cleansing, perform the ritual to active your amulet on a Sunday. Hold the amulet in your hands and recite the prayer of the Fourteen Holy Helpers.

After the first prayer of healing, you can also say the prayer that relates to the issue you wish to address.

In order to reprogram your amulet, carry out a cleansing as described on page 67.

- Keeping the Holy Helpers amulet with you on your person will help with acute complaints.

- When threaded with the recommended crystals and worn around the neck, the amulet will be endowed with significant protective powers and will bring you joy and happiness.

- To combat anxiety, depression, or nightmares, place the amulet next to your bed or under your pillow. It will help with the letting go of grief, anger, and similar negative feelings.

- The amulet is also a protective talisman for your house or apartment and it can be carried in your vehicle.

Asking angels and saints for help

Some people are surrounded by choirs of angels and hosts of ascended Masters, beings that are ready to help us and wish to be with us. However, a universal law forbids intervention in the life of a human by angels or saints unless prayers have been said to invoke their help. Times of mortal danger when our life here on Earth has not yet reached its end are the only exception to this.

Angels and saints hear the prayers of our heart and can be called upon at any time. They are there for each and every one of us equally, we simply need to invoke their help. There are two ways in which to do this: a prayer of supplication or a "petition." It does not matter which method you choose; both will be effective as long as the request is made with a pure heart.

Write down your concerns
Hold nothing back. Make a note of all your anxieties and worries.

Internal conversation
Simply concentrating on a saint in your thoughts is enough to call upon them.

Speak out loud
You can also address the saints and angels aloud.

Sensing the presence of angels and saints

Their presence might be revealed as a gentle touch on the face, shoulders, arms, or hands. Some people experience a sensation of warmth.

Seeing angels and saints

A sparkling light, just a glint of white, blue, or green glimpsed from the corner of your eye, is a sign that they are nearby. You might also see a glowing shadow, moving quickly.

Hearing angels and saints

Hearing a saint or angel is like the first thought that comes to mind before you begin to think consciously. It is like a flash of inspiration or a spontaneous idea, and is most likely to take place in the peace and quiet of the natural world or during meditation.

Angels and saints are not alone in coming to offer consolation and help, spirit guides do so, too. These are generally people who have passed on but are still providing loving support, perhaps your grandmother or grandfather, or great-grandmother. They often manifest as a scent, so you might realize that they are with you by their perfume, aftershave, or the fragrance of their favorite flower.

How to formulate prayers of supplication

Your request must be formulated clearly and unambiguously. However, "I want..." is not the right approach. It signals desire, and "I want, doesn't get" as the saying goes. You are far more likely to be left waiting in line for ever. Be really honest and frank with yourself. Learn to turn your thoughts and feelings from negative to positive.

Examples:

Saint (name), give me the strength to find a way to achieve (desired outcome).

Saint (name), help me to (desired outcome).

Saint (name), from now on I shall (desired outcome).

Saint (name), I am now starting to (desired outcome).

These requests should contain all your energy and should always close with the sentence:

"So shall it be."

Now recite the Our Father (the Lord's Prayer, see overleaf). It has great power. Having been translated into every language, it can be found in all the religions of the world. Recite it sincerely and you will be heard.

In my experience, events that could be described as miracles have often taken place.

Our Father

Our Father, who art in heaven,
Hallowed be thy name.
Thy kingdom come.
Thy will be done,
On Earth as it is in heaven.
Give us this day our daily bread.
And forgive us our trespasses,
as we forgive those who trespass against us.
And lead us not into temptation,
but deliver us from evil.
For thine is the kingdom, the power
and the glory, for ever and ever.
Amen.

How to formulate a petition

A petition should be written in your own handwriting to ensure that your energy is contained within it.

Take a blank, unlined sheet of paper and follow the same procedure as with the prayers of supplication:

- For general requests, use white paper.

- For affairs of the heart, use pink or bright red paper.

- For financial matters, use green paper.

- For professional, communicational matters, use blue paper.

Always end your petition with the powerful sentence:

"So shall it be."

Give thanks for the granting of your wish and sign your name.

You could include a relevant object, such as a coin for financial matters, a photograph of the person who is dear to you for a relationship issue, an earring whose partner you have lost. You could also draw symbols or signs on the petition that please you and give you a good feeling.

Feel free to design your petition entirely as you wish. Place everything in an envelope, write the date on it, and insert it in a small casket or between the pages of your favorite book.

Do not forget to recite the Our Father.

Once your wish has come true, burn the petition to release the energy back into the universe.

SAMPLE PETITIONS

HELP IN MATTERS OF THE HEART

For romantic affairs of the heart, use a sheet of pink or red paper and perhaps add a few rose petals, a photograph of the relevant person, or another personal object.

You will find the appropriate saint or ascended Master for the issue you intend to address on pages 82–83. In terms of romance, it would be Saint Cornelius or Saint Valentine, or call upon both if you prefer.

Below is an example of how the petition might look if you have to date only exchanged glances with a person you would like to get to know, if there has been some recognizable interest, or just general communication with a strong attraction on both sides (and on a spiritual level).

1. Petition (date)

Saint Cornelius, help us, (your name and that of the other person), to become a couple. Aid us both in finding an easy way to become close and let love enter our lives.

Please let my wish come true.

So shall it be.

Thank you.

(*Signature*)

2.   *Petition (date)*

Saint Cornelius and Saint Valentine, please help me, (your name), to attract a suitable partner into my life. He/she should love me sincerely and loyally, stay with me in the good times and the bad, just as I shall love him/her sincerely and stay with him/her in good times and bad. This is my deepest desire (add any details and feelings).
Please let my wish come true.

So shall it be.

Thank you.

(*Signature*)

Now design your petition as you prefer, perhaps adding drawings of hearts or scattering it with rose petals. Place the petition in an envelope before reciting the Our Father once.

HELP WITH CAREERS

Petition (date)

Use a sheet of blue paper for professional matters, examinations, and so on. Choose from among the Holy Helpers who are patron saints of the professions as relevant.

On the following page is a sample petition for attending an interview for a job you are particularly keen to secure. It might, for example, be a good fit with a part of your skill set or it might suit your career ambitions perfectly.

Help with preparing for an interview for a new job

Saint Catherine, help me by making sure my interview with (company) on (date) is a success. I passionately want this job because I believe I could be a great asset to the firm. Saint Catherine, help me by making sure I like my new job and that I am able to deal with the work easily and find it enjoyable. Pleasant and friendly coworkers are also important to me.

May my wish come true.

So shall it be.

Thank you.

(*Signature*)

Place the petition in an envelope before reciting the Our Father once.

Keep the petition somewhere safe or between the pages of your favorite book. Once your wish has come true, burn the petition to release the energy back into the universe.

Belief and trust

All of creation, all the angels, saints, ascended Masters, and the light beings that hold the universe in readiness for us would never wish to harm or hurt us. They carry out what we desire, believe, or focus on without bias, which is why it is important to pay attention to what we think and say.

Naturally, the Universe wants things to go well for us and to fulfill our every desire: "Your wish is my command." Unfortunately, almost none of us think to ask, "Hello everyone up there, what do think of this?" As a result, they are not able (or permitted) to go over our heads and intervene, except when we pray intensively for someone or something. Prayer chains or praying in groups or in power places such as churches, chapels, or holy sites are very successful.

Prayers are like a devotional pause in our hectic lives, a switching-off from noise, hassle, and stress. Learn to trust at its most primal level, become self-aware once more and treat your body with great love. Make yourself comfortable, light a candle, and allow it to rest and relax. You are important and a part of the Whole. Believe and trust, and help will be yours.

Epilogue

A T ONE TIME no house was complete without an image of a guardian angel, a statue of a saint, or a crucifix. Much has been lost over the years. We have forgotten how to pray and have ceased to care whether we have any such images in our home that could deliver strength and power.

People often pursue a single goal in life: to carve out a career and make money, with no regard for who or what is left behind in the process. This "me first" society has consumed all our attention for years, with the ultimate aim being to fight our way to the front of the line. However, our many and diverse experiences are teaching us to think again, and we are now reconsidering and looking at ways of incorporating divine power into our daily lives once more. We remember the ascended Masters, angels, and familiar spirits and consider asking them for help. Everyday magic is returning to our lives, but what exactly is magic?

Magic is as old as the world; we encounter the tools for magic everywhere: in old documents and in oral traditions, in items found in archeological excavations across the globe. Making sacrifices and lighting candles are also a part of magic, as is the burning of incense with resins and herbs. Magic is practiced wherever religion and faith unite. Be observant as you go about your everyday life and you will see signs of magic everywhere: Saint Christopher medals hanging in car windscreens, crucifix pendants on chains, talismans, wedding rings, and many more. These symbols are a natural part of our everyday life, of course, but they are all examples of magical action.

Magic is an ancient knowledge, a link between human beings and the universe that can help us transform our lives.

Rituals cannot rid the world of all its problems, of course, but a ritual performed with love is a practical way of encouraging the desired outcome. The fundamental rule is to do as you wish while doing no harm to others.

Christiane Stamm (née Herber)

Appendix

The Fourteen Holy Helpers as patron saints of professions

IN CENTURIES PAST, and even today, many people believe in the power and protection of the saints. Listed below are the professions that come under the particular protection of each saint. Some saints share stewardship of a vocation, so nurses can call upon both Saint Margaret or Saint Pantaleon, for example.

Saint Christopher
Truck drivers, travelers, gardeners, bookbinders, athletes, seafarers, carpenters, motor mechanics, postal workers, delivery drivers, printers.

Saint Blaise
Musicians, bakers, millers, plasterers, tailors, shoemakers, painters, varnishers, watchmakers.

Saint Margaret of Antioch
Farmers, shepherds, midwives, livestock breeders, nurses, carers.

Saint Catherine of Alexandria
Philosophers, teachers, students, lawyers, notaries, hairdressers, librarians, seamstresses, office workers, publishers, authors, interpreters, retailers.

Saint Barbara
Miners, architects, geologists, archeologists, bricklayers, roofers, electricians, butchers, cooks, farmers, stonemasons, internet professionals, IT workers, call center workers.

Saint George
Hikers, soldiers, farmers, scouts, artists, blacksmiths, lathe operators, milling machine operators, toolmakers, all metal-working professions.

Saint Pantaleon
Physicians, midwives, nurses, carers, veterinary surgeons, healers.

Saint Denis
Police officers, detectives, security personnel.

Saint Cyriacus
Wine-growers, unemployed people, people in physically demanding jobs, warehouse employees.

Saint Eustace
Foresters, hunters, lumberjacks, forest workers, grocers, plumbers, bakers, butchers.

Saint Agathius
Soldiers, police officers, security personnel.

Saint Giles
Housewives and mothers, shepherds, hunters, educators, curative educators.

Saint Erasmus
Woodturners, joiners, seafarers, all wood-working professionals.

Saint Vitus
Innkeepers, pharmacists, actors, brewers, miners, all media sector professionals, television, radio, journalists, photographers, chemists, lab technicians.

Brief biographies of the patron saints

Saint Agathius (Acacius of Byzantium)
Saint's day: May 8
Born in Turkey
Died 303/304 CE in modern-day Istanbul (Turkey)

The name Agathius means "God holds."

According to the legend, Agathius was a soldier in the imperial Roman army. After suffering greatly, persecuted and tortured, he was executed during the reign of Emperor Maximian.

Saint Barbara
Saint's day: (Catholic and Protestant) December 4
Born in Nicomedia (modern-day Turkey) in the 3rd century CE
Died circa 306 CE in Nicomedia

The name Barbara means "the foreign one."

Barbara was an extremely beautiful and intelligent woman. However, her pagan father was jealous and possessive, and locked her in a tower to prevent her from marrying.

One day, when her father was away on a journey, Barbara climbed into a pagan sacrificial pit and John the Baptist appeared to her. Filled with the Holy Spirit, she was baptized and became a Christian.

Saint Blaise (Blase)
Saint's day: February 3
Born in Sebaste (modern-day Turkey) in the 3rd century CE
Died circa 316 CE in Turkey

Legend has it that Blaise lived in a cave during the time that Christians were being persecuted. The wild animals of the forest would bring him food and Blaise would heal their wounds.

One day, Blaise was thrown into a lake. He made the sign of the cross and Christ appeared to him. When Blaise and Christ reached the shore, their feet were still dry, while the persecutors of Blaise had drowned in the floodwaters.

Blaise was a physician and a bishop. His one wish before he died was that all those suffering from a throat/neck complaint would be heard if they asked for help. A voice from above assured him that it would be so.

From this arose the symbol used in the blessing of throats, two candles held in the shape of a St. Andrew's cross.

Saint Catherine of Alexandria
Saint's day: (Catholic and Protestant) November 25
Born in Cyprus (?)
Died circa 306 CE in Alexandria (Egypt)

The name Catherine means "the pure."

The beautiful and educated Catherine was the daughter of King Costus of Cyprus. She spurned every man who asked for her hand in marriage, however, and was informed by a hermit that her true husband was Jesus. She was baptized and experienced a vision in which Jesus placed an engagement ring on her finger. She then became what is known as a "consecrated virgin."

As a result of her hostile attitude toward Maxentius, the Roman emperor, who had attempted to win her hand, Catherine was ultimately broken on the wheel and then beheaded.

Saint Christopher

Saint's day: (Catholic) July 25, (Protestant) July 24
Born in Canaan or Lycia (Turkey)
Died circa 250 CE

Legends concerning Saint Christopher abound, the best known among them being that of the "Christ bearer," from which the saint's name is derived.

Christopher is described as a tall, powerfully built man, who undertook the task of carrying people across a river with the aid of a large staff. One day, he encountered a small boy who wished to be carried across. As Christopher bore the child across the river, his burden grew increasingly heavy and finally become almost unbearable. Once they reached the bank, the child said to him, "You bore more than the world on your shoulders." Christopher then recognized the child to be Christ.

The boy dipped the man under the water and baptized him with the name Christopher, further commanding him to push his staff into the earth. By next morning, a palm tree had grown up out of his staff down into the earth.

Saint Cyriacus

Saint's day: (Catholic and Protestant) August 8
Place and date of birth unknown
Died 305 CE, probably in Rome

The name Cyriacus means "of the Lord."

Cyriacus was anointed a deacon in Rome in around 300 CE. He was summoned to Artemisia, daughter of Emperor Diocletian. Artemisia was said to be possessed by the devil, but Cyriacus healed and baptized her.

Soon after this, Cyriacus was called again, this time to Persia to free the daughter of the Persian king from possession. After he had freed her, he baptized both the daughter and her parents. He was beheaded by pagans after Diocletian abdicated the imperial throne.

Saint Denis (Dionysius)
Saint's day: (Catholic and Protestant) October 9
Born in Italy
Died after 250 CE in modern-day Paris

According to the story that has been passed down to us, Denis was the first bishop of Paris. Accompanied by six other bishops, he was sent to Gaul (an ancient region that included modern-day France) as a missionary.

After he had begun preaching there, he was arrested and beheaded. The legend says that after being executed, he took his head in his hands and walked to the place where he wished to be buried.

Saint Erasmus (Elmo)
Saint's day: June 2
Born in Syria, beginning of the 3rd century CE
Died 303 CE in Campania (Italy)

The name Erasmus means "beloved."

Erasmus was bishop of Antioch around 300 CE. He went into hiding for seven years, during which time he prayed for the Christians who were undergoing great persecution.

It is said that Erasmus was placed in a cauldron of boiling oil. A few drops splashed out and hit the emperor, who begged Erasmus for help. Erasmus climbed out of the boiling oil entirely unharmed.

He went on to baptize thousands of people and kept the population safe from disaster and harm with his prayers. Erasmus lived as a pastor and was visited by the Archangel Michael at the hour of his death.

Saint Eustace (Placidus)

Saint's day: September 20
Place and date of birth unknown
Died 118 CE, probably in Rome

The name Eustace means "the steadfast one" and "fruitful."

One day, during a hunt, a stag appeared to Eustace on a rock, with a vision of the crucified Christ between its antlers. Eustace heard Christ say to him, "I am Christ, who created heaven and earth, who divided the darkness and commanded the light to shine."

Jesus appeared once more to Eustace and his wife, whereupon he had himself, his wife, and his children baptized. He was then given the name Eustace.

Saint George the Martyr

Saint's day: (Catholic and Protestant) April 23
Born in Turkey in the 3rd century CE
Died circa 305 CE in Lod (Israel)

The name George means "the countryman."

Many legends surround this saint. One tells of how a sorcerer gave George a poisoned drink, but he made the sign of the cross over it and so remained unharmed.

On another occasion, even when molten lead from a barrel was poured over him, he was not injured. George then converted to Christianity, kneeled down, and began to pray. Fire immediately fell from heaven, burning pagan idols and temples.

As a result of his deeds, George was seen as a symbol of chivalry. Horses are still blessed and processions on horseback are held on Saint George's Day, honoring an ancient tradition.

Saint Giles (Gilles)
Saint's day: September 1
Born circa 640 CE in Athens
Died September 1, 720 CE, at St. Gilles Abbey (France)

The name Giles means "the wearer of goatskin" or "shield bearer."

The legend says that Giles, who came from a noble house, lived first as a hermit. One day during a hunt, he was hit by an arrow fired by the king of the Visigoths.

After recovering, he was allowed to found a monastery. He went on to found the Benedictine Abbey of St. Gilles near the town of Arles in France, in around 680 CE. Giles was to remain abbot until his death.

Saint Margaret of Antioch (Saint Marina the Great Martyr)
Saint's day: (Catholic and Protestant) July 20
Born in Antioch in Pisidia (modern-day Turkey)
Died 305 CE in Turkey

The name Margaret means "the pearl."

According to the story that has been handed down, Margaret was the daughter of a pagan priest, but her father disowned her when he became aware that she had converted to the Christian faith.

Margaret was plunged into boiling oil and burned with torches, but neither affected her and she remained uninjured. The people were so in awe that they converted to Christianity and were baptized.

Saint Pantaleon (Panteleimon)
Saint's day: (Catholic) July 27
Born in Nicomedia (modern-day Turkey) in the second half of the
3rd century CE
Died circa 305 CE

The name Panteleimon means "all compassionate."

Legend has it that Pantaleon was the son of a Christian and a pagan. He was admired for the healing powers he possessed even as a child. In the presence of his father, he made a blind man see again by praying to Christ. Upon witnessing this event, his father converted to Christianity.

The Eastern Orthodox Church honors Pantaleon as a martyr to this day, and he is considered one of the Holy Doctors of the Church, saints recognized as having made a significant contribution to doctrine.

Saint Vitus (Guy)
Saint's day: June 15
Born in Mazzara (modern-day Mazara, Italy)
Died 304 CE in Lucania (modern-day Southern Italy)

The name Vitus derives from Latin and means "wood."

Vitus was born the son of a pagan and during his childhood was constantly beaten by his father for refusing to give up his Christian faith. Vitus also suffered a beating later in life, but the arms of those who hit him withered.

Vitus began to pray to Christ and healed his tormentors. His father locked him in a room with a girl and watched through the keyhole. However, his father was then struck blind and was healed only through the prayers of his son.

Saints and ascended Masters

INVOKING A SAINT or an ascended Master helps people to deal with difficult or threatening situations more easily, or even to avert them in advance. Call upon the saints listed below to make daily concerns and issues easier to handle or to heal a given situation. The short biographies also reveal why these people were canonized.

against alcoholism	St. John the Baptist
against nightmares	St. Franca Visalta (Franca of Piacenza)
accusations, legal matters, authorities	St. Dorothea, St. Jeanne-Marie de Maille
hopeless situations and issues	Fourteen Holy Helpers
career choices	St. Aloysius (Luigi) de Gonzaga
in the event of theft	St. Edigna of Puch
against theft	St. Nicholas of Myra, St. Peter, St. Philip of Zell, St. Gervase, St. Protase
for discovery of theft	St. Helena
to recover stolen objects	St. Nicholas of Myra
for lost items	St. Anthony of Padua
all affairs of the heart	St. Cornelius, St. Valentine of Rome

for a good marriage	St. Ursula of Cologne
for happiness in marriage	St. Andrew (the Apostle)
to find a spouse	St. Andrew (the Apostle)
to help with marital problems	St. Gangulphus
for separated spouses	St. Philip of Arundel
childlessness	St. Agatha of Sicily
conflict	St. Barnabas
looking for a home	St. Joseph of Nazareth
to mediate differences of opinion	St. Expeditus (patron saint of schoolchildren and students)
during court cases	St. Ivo (Yves) of Kermartin
defamation and misfortune	St. Susanna
fire hazards	Fourteen Holy Helpers
evil spirits	Fourteen Holy Helpers
examinations	St. Expeditus
successful examinations	St. Joseph of Cupertino
study	St. Acca of Hexham, St. Ambrose of Milan
traffic, journeys	St. Christopher
torments of the soul and spiritual crises	St. Anastasia
financial matters	St. Corona (Stephana)
lottery	St. Corona (Stephana)
prophecies, spirituality, forgiveness	St. Pio
the internet	St. Isidor of Seville

You will notice that the list does not include a surname for the saints or ascended persons. This is because they are either known only by the name that has been handed down to us, or because the saint is so well known that the surname is irrelevant.

Brief biographies of the saints and ascended Masters

ALTHOUGH THESE BIOGRAPHIES are brief, they still reveal the immense steadfastness, courage, stamina, perseverance, love, and devotion that characterize the lives and fates of these individuals. As you read, you may experience an especially intense sensation, similar to a feeling of connection. If so, you can be confident that this vibration will be of particular benefit.

Saint Acca of Hexham
Saint's day: February 19
Born circa 660 CE, England
Died circa October 20, 742 CE, Hexham (England)

Acca accompanied Saint Wilfrid of York to Rome in 692 and was appointed abbot of Saint Andrew's Monastery at Hexham upon his return. After Wilfrid's death, Acca became his successor and was appointed bishop of Hexham. His constant concern was to preserve the teachings of Rome.

Saint Agatha of Sicily
Saint's day: February 5
Born circa 225 CE, Catania (Sicily, Italy)
Died circa 251 CE, Catania

Her name means "the good."

Agatha was a beautiful noblewoman and attracted the attentions of Quintanius, the Roman prefect, who wanted to marry her. When she rebuffed him as she was a Christian, Quintianus took advantage of the Christian persecutions to denounce her; she was arrested and sent to a brothel to be seduced. She was tortured and her breasts were torn off with pincers. Incarcerated in a dungeon, during the night Saint Peter appeared to her with a healing salve, but she refused all aid and died the next day.

Saint Aloysius (Luigi) de Gonzaga

Saint's day: June 21
Born March 9, 1568, Italy
Died June 21, 1591, Rome

His name means "the wholly wise" and "renowned warrior."

Luigi was brought up by his mother to be very devout and in his tenth year he decided to live a life of constant self-denial. He entered a Jesuit order in 1585, where he spent his time studying theology. Luigi mainly devoted himself to the poor and young people, who could turn to him with any kind of problem. While caring for the sick during a plague epidemic, he also contracted the disease and died.

Saint Ambrose of Milan

Saint's day: December 7
Born 339 CE, Trier (Rhineland-Palatinate, Germany)
Died April 4, 397 CE, Milan (Italy)

His name means "the immortal."

Ambrose studied theology and as a pastor took great care of the poor. Surrounded by people wherever he went, he became a gifted preacher. Ambrose defended the independence of the church against the state and was awarded the title "Church Father" in 1295.

Saint Anastasia

Saint's day: December 25
Born mid-3rd century CE, Rome
Died December 25, circa 304 CE

Her name means "resurrection."

According to the stories that have been passed down, Anastasia was the sister of Constantine, the Roman emperor, and was betrothed to a pagan man against her will. She took care of imprisoned Christians and was later incarcerated herself, before being banished to an island. Her death was said to have taken place during the first hour of the Christmas festival. By the time of the Middle Ages, centuries later, Anastasia had become one of the most venerated saints in the Christian world.

Saint Andrew (the Apostle)

Saint's day: November 30
Born 1st century BCE, Bethsaida (Israel)
Died November 30, 60/70 CE, Greece

Andrew was the first disciple that Jesus called to his side. According to the legend, Andrew freed Matthew from prison and restored his sight. Andrew is said to have performed many miracles and healings. However, a city governor whom Andrew was unable to convert had the apostle tortured and crucified on a diagonal cross, where he died after suffering for two days. There is unfortunately no clear indication of the country in which this took place.

Saint Anthony of Padua

Saint's day: September 16
Born circa 1195, Lisbon (Portugal)
Died June 13, 1231, Padua (Italy)

His name means "the foremost one."

Anthony studied in Lisbon and was admitted to the priesthood. In 1220 he joined the Franciscan order at Saint Anthony's Monastery in Olivais, in Portugal. His oratory skills brought him extraordinary renown, with those who heard his speeches feeeling profoundly drawn to him. Legend has it that he performed many miracles and he was named "Ark of the Testament" by Pope Gregory.

Saint Barnabas
Saint's day: June 11
Born in Cyprus
Died 61 CE, Cyprus

His name means "son of consolation."

Although named Joseph at birth, he was known as Barnabas among the apostles. He lived in faith and accompanied Saint Paul on his missionary journey to Cyprus. Barnabas is said to have healed the sick by placing upon them the Gospel of Saint Matthew, which he always carried with him.

Saint Christopher
(one of the Fourteen Holy Helpers, see page 86)

Saint Cornelius
Saint's day: September 16
Born in Rome
Died in June 253 CE, Italy

His name means "strong as a horn."

Cornelius was elected bishop of Rome (the pope) in 251 CE. According to one legend that originates in the North Rhine-Westphalia region of Germany, an artist wished to marry the daughter of a lord of the manor. The lord said that he would permit the two to marry only if the pope blessed their union. Cornelius leaned down from the altar and blessed the happy couple.

Saint Corona (Stephana)
Saint's day: May 14
Born circa 160 CE, Egypt
Died circa 177 CE

Her name means "crown."

Little is known about the life and death of Corona. She was the wife of a martyr and died in great torment and suffering at the age of sixteen. Several towns and cities in Germany and Austria have been named after her, and until 1924 the smallest unit of Austrian currency, known as the Krone, was also named after her.

Saint Dorothea
Saint's day: February 6
Born circa 290 CE, Caesarea (Cappadocia, Turkey)
Died circa 304 or 287 CE, Caesarea

Her name means "God's gift."

Dorothea joins Barbara, Margaret, and Catherine as one of the "four capital virgins." According to legend, when Dorothea was due to be married, she declared that she wished to live as a Christian and was brought before the court. She was tortured, but her wounds healed overnight in a miraculous way and she remained unharmed.

Saint Edigna of Puch
Saint's day: February 26
Born in the 10th century in France
Died February 26, 1109, Puch (modern-day Fürstenfeldbruck, Germany)

Her name means "one who fights for possessions."

According to legend, Edigna fled in an oxcart when she was about to be forced to marry against her will. Her flight ended in the German region of Bavaria, where she lived in a hollow tree for thirty-five years. She taught the people who lived nearby how to read and write and took care of their daily needs and concerns.

Saint Expeditus
Saint's day: April 19
Born in Armenia
Died 303 CE, Malatya (Turkey)

His name means "the liberated, ready for battle."

Expeditus is venerated around the Pacific, possibly as the result of a linguistic confusion. A shrine with relics and a statue was sent from Rome to the Monastery of Saint Paul, marked "Spedito"(shipped), but the nuns thought it was the name of the saint and the cult surrounding Saint Expeditus was born. It became increasingly popular and today many shrines can be found in the mountains and forests of Reunion Island, and Expeditus is considered by Hindus to be a reincarnation of their god Vishnu.

Saint Franca Visalta (Franca of Piacenza)
Saint's day: April 25
Born 1173, Piacenza (Italy)
Died April 25, 1218, Pittolo (Italy)

Her name means "the Frankish woman."

Franca brokered peace between her home city of Piacenza in Italy and the pope in 1206. She lived and worked as a Benedictine nun and was abbess of San Sisto Monastery in Piacenza from 1198.

Saint Frances Xavier Cabrini
Saint's day: December 22
Born July 15, 1850, Milan (Italy)
Died December 22, 1917, USA

Her name means "Frankish."

The youngest of thirteen children, Frances was already taking care of disadvantaged children in her youth. She founded an order of missionary sisters in 1880. Several years later, in 1888, Pope Leo XIII sent Frances to the USA, where she would work up to twenty hours a day at schools, hospitals, and orphanages. Frances became a US citizen in 1909.

Saint Gangulphus
Saint's day: May 11
Born in Burgundy (France)
Died around 760 CE, Burgundy

His name means "attacking wolf."

Shortly after his marriage Gangulphus discovered that his wife was betraying him with a priest. Although his wife denied this, Gangulphus banished the adulterous priest from the country. However, his wife asked her lover to return and subsequently charged him with killing her husband, who had by now been slain. When Gangulphus was buried, several miracles took place, but his wife met these only with scorn. Her lover died soon after of a serious disease.

Saint Gervase

Saint's day: June 19
Place and date of birth unknown
Died around 300 CE, Milan (Italy)

His name means "servant spear."

Very little is known about the life of Saint Gervase. Bishop Ambrose of Milan discovered his remains and a blind man who was helping to rebury the bones suddenly recovered his sight. Bishop Ambrose was buried beside Gervase.

Saint Helena

Saint's day: August 18
Born around 249 CE, Drepanon (Turkey)
Died circa 18 August 329 CE, Nicodemia (modern-day Turkey)

Her name means "shining light."

According to the legend, in around 289 Helena was banished by her husband Emperor Constantius, because of her lowly background, but she was to remain influential. She lived in what is now Trier for some time. Helena played a leading role in acquiring the "Holy Tunic" of Jesus and the bones of Saint Matthew and is now patron saint of the cities of Trier and Frankfurt (both in Germany) and Pesaro (in Italy).

Saint Isidor of Seville

Saint's day: April 4
Born circa 560 CE, Spain
Died April 4, 636 CE, Seville (Spain)

His name means "gift of the goddess Isis."

Isidor entered a monastery as a young man and become abbot at the age
of thirty. He attached particular importance to the education of priests
and established schools and libraries. He became the national saint of
Spain and was canonized in 1598.

Saint Ivo (Yves) of Kermartin

Saint's day: May 19
Born October 17, 1253, Brittany (France)
Died May 19, 1303, Kermartin (France)

His name means "like yew wood."

Yves began his study of theology, philosophy, and the law in Paris at the
age of fourteen. He entered the priesthood in 1284, before giving up
his vocation as a pastor after several years and devoting himself exclu-
sively to the poor and suffering. His selfless attitude earned him the title
"Advocate of the Poor."

Saint Jeanne-Marie de Maille

Saint's day: March 28
Born April 14, 1331, Roche Saint-Quentin (France)
Died March 28, 1414, Tours (France)

Her name means "God is merciful."

Jeanne-Marie was the daughter of Baron de Maille and decided at the
young age of eleven to lead a life led by faith. She married at sixteen, but
her husband died of the plague in 1362, whereupon Jeanne-Marie joined
a monastery and lived as an anchoress. She was greatly admired for the
advice she gave to rich and poor alike.

Saint Joan of Arc
Saint's day: May 30
Born January 6, 1412, France
Died May 30, 1431, Rouen (France)

Her name means "God is gracious."

At the age of fourteen, Joan heard "voices."The Archangel Michael and the Holy Helpers Saint Catherine and Saint Margaret appeared to her, commanding her to liberate France from the English. An emancipated and self-aware young woman, she followed her inner voice and helped Charles VII to his coronation in 1421. She was accused of many things, including sorcery, cruelty, and arrogance, but despite the accusations made no confession and was executed as a heretic.

Saint John the Baptist
Saint's day: June 24
Born June 24, 1st century BCE, near Jerusalem (Israel)
Died after 29 CE, Jerusalem

His name means "God is merciful."

In many legends, John, an itinerant preacher of the gospel, is represented as an angel, with a place at Jesus Christ's left hand. Saint John's Day is still celebrated on June 24 to this day and has been grafted onto the Celtic summer festival, when the light of the sun will be victorious over darkness. The plant Saint-John's-wort blooms around this time and is said to have protective properties.

Saint Joseph of Cupertino
Saint's day: September 18
Born 1603, Cupertino (Italy)
Died 18 September 1663, Cupertino

Joseph was a Franciscan monk who was known for the time he spent "flying" or levitating. He was venerated by the people and performed many miracles, but this did not meet with the approval of the highest church authorities and he was sent to a remote monastery.

Saint Joseph of Nazareth

Saint's day: March 19
Born 1st century BCE, Nazareth (Lower Galilee, Israel)
Died circa 16 CE

His name means "God has added him."

The Old Testament tells us that Joseph was descended from the house of King David, that he lived and worked as a carpenter, and that he was engaged to Mary, the mother of Jesus. Joseph was having doubts about his bride's faithfulness, but when an angel appeared, telling him that Mary was pregnant by the "Holy Spirit," his doubts were dispelled. Joseph and Mary traveled to Bethlehem to take part in a census called by the authorities and Jesus was born in a stable there. "Saint Joseph the Worker" is celebrated in many countries on May 1, a feast day introduced by Pope Pius XII in 1955.

Saint Nicholas of Myra

Saint's day: December 6
Born circa 280/286 CE in modern-day Turkey
Died circa 343/344 CE, Myra (modern-day Turkey)

His name means "victory of the people."

Nicholas was anointed a priest at the age of nineteen and took office as an abbot near his home town. There are many legends concerning him. For example, he was once able to save three men who were condemned to death by appearing to the emperor in a vision and taking the ax from the executioner's hand.

Nicholas remains one of the best-known saints to this day, achieving renown through his helpful and unselfish manner. He will always be remembered through the custom of giving gifts to children on Saint Nicholas's Day.

Saint Peter (the Apostle)

Saint's day: June 29
Born circa 1st century BCE, Bethsaida (Israel)
Died circa 64 CE, Rome

His name means "the rock."

Peter, also known as Simon Peter, lived as a fisherman with his wife and children beside the Sea of Galilee. According to the Gospel of St. Mark, Peter and his brother Andrew, who was also a disciple of John the Baptist, were called to join Jesus's group of disciples. Peter would heal people wherever he went, and the sick would become well again even if they had been simply touched by his shadow. Peter gave a sermon at Pentecost and a lame man was able to walk again. According to the legend, Peter guards the gates of heaven with his keys, and the Roman Catholic popes are considered to be his direct successors.

Saint Philip of Arundel

Saint's day: October 19
Born June 28, 1557, London
Died October 19, 1595, London

Philip Howard was the son of Thomas, duke of Norfolk, who was executed for plotting against Queen Elizabeth I. Philip's godfather sent him to Cambridge University and he became earl of Arundel in February 1580. His wife, Anne Dacre, converted to Roman Catholicism in 1581 and Philip followed in 1584. This news was not well received at court and in the wake of Philip's having read a mass for the success of the Spanish fleet's invasion of England in 1588, he was tried in 1589 and found guilty of treason. He was condemned to death but never executed.

Saint Philip of Zell

Saint's day: May 3
Born 8th century CE, England
Died 8th century CE, Zell (Rhineland-Palatinate, Germany)

His name means "horse-loving."

Philip was anointed a priest in Rome. On his journey home, he settled near Worms, in Germany, where St. Michael's Chapel still stands to this day as the focal point of the town of Zell. Many miracles have occurred at Philip's grave.

Saint Pio (Padre Pio)

Saint's day: September 23
Born May 25, 1887, Pietrelcina (Italy)
Died September 23, 1968

His name means "pious."

Having joined the Capuchin order at the age of sixteen, he was given the name Pio. Despite suffering from tuberculosis, he studied theology and entered the priesthood in 1910. Stigmata (the wounds of Christ) became visible on his body in 1918 and remained until his death. Padre Pio began healing in 1940 by the laying on of hands. He also had prophetic gifts, foretelling the appointment of Karol Wojtyla as pope (Karol would go on to become Pope John Paul II), along with the attempt on John Paul's life. Padre Pio was canonized by John Paul II in June 2002.

Saint Protase

Saint's day: June 19
Place and date of birth unknown
Died circa 300 CE, Milan (Italy)

His name means "the foremost."

Twin brothers Protase and Gervase achieved renown as Milan's first martyrs. When the two brothers refused to deny Jesus Christ and pray to other gods, Count Astacius had them beheaded. However, little else is known of their lives.

Saint Susanna

Saint's day: August 11
Place and date of birth unknown
Died circa 304 CE, Rome

Her name means "the lily."

Susanna's father was a priest and her uncle was Pope Gaius. She is said to have been strangled in her parents' house after refusing to marry the son of Emperor Diocletian. Excavations in Rome have revealed a house dating from the 3rd century, where one wall features images of Saint Susanna. Her relics are still held in the church of Santa Susanna in Rome.

Saint Ursula of Cologne

Saint's day: October 21
Born 4th century CE in England
Died 4th century CE, Cologne (Germany)

Her name means "little bear."

Ursula was the daughter of King Maurus, a Christian, and decided at a very early age to live as a virgin. Her father promised his daughter in marriage to Etherius, the son of an English prince, but Ursula asked for three years' grace, during which time Etherius was to be instructed in the Christian faith and baptized. According to the story, this subsequently took place. Ursula is said to have met her death at the point of a Hun's spear, thereby becoming a martyr and the patron saint of the people of the German city of Cologne.

Saint Valentine of Rome
Saint's day: October 21
Born in England
Died circa 304 or 451 CE in Cologne (Germany)

His name means "strong and healthy."

According to the legend, although he lived as a poor priest, Valentine was nonetheless held in high regard. He would give flowers from his garden to those who sought his assistance and support, and was always ready to listen to their troubles. Valentine was beheaded for marrying couples according to the Christian rite. He is remembered to this day, when lovers give the gift of flowers on February 14 (Saint Valentine's Day).

Bibliography

Gienger, Michael; Goebel, Joachim, *Gem Water*, Earthdancer 2008

Gienger, Michael, *Healing Crystals: the A–Z Guide to 555 Gemstones*, Earthdancer 2014

Mohr, Baerbel, *The Cosmic Ordering Service: A Guide to Realizing Your Dreams*, Hampton Roads Publishing 2001

Murphy, Dr. Joseph, *The Power of Your Subconscious Mind*, Wilder Publications 2008

www. heiligenlexikon.de

I would be glad to answer any questions you might have about the book at the following email address:

chrisherber@gmx.de

Christiane Stamm

About the author

Christiane Stamm (née Herber) was born in 1964 and works with young people and adults as a commercial trainer and relaxation teacher. She married in 2017 and now lives in Germany's Saarland region with her husband Wolfgang, her grown-up children, and three pets. In addition to writing, her great hobby is making soap.

For further information and to request a book catalog contact:
Inner Traditions, One Park Street, Rochester, Vermont 05767

Earthdancer Books is an Inner Traditions imprint
Phone: +1-800-246-8648, customerservice@innertraditions.com
www.earthdancerbooks.com • www.innertraditions.com

AN INNER TRADITIONS IMPRINT